Leadership *for* Learning

M J BROMLEY

ISBN-13: 978-1478347941
ISBN-10: 1478347945

FOR NICKI & STUART

BE Publishing
England, UK

First published in 2012

CONTENTS

INTRODUCTION

Why should you read this book?

Countless books have been written on the subject of school leadership: some claim to know the *philosophy* of school leadership; others promise to share the *secret* of school leadership. Many of these books have value; they contain nuggets of useful information based on detailed research. But most are theoretical; they are not practical. Once read, they are rarely again consulted. As good as they are, school leaders do not turn to them when they need ideas or inspiration.

The **ABC of School Improvement** is different: it is a practical handbook for busy senior leaders – a book of ideas which can be put into practice, which can be dipped into when help and advice are needed most. This author is different, too: I am not a university professor; I am a senior leader working in schools every day. I have worked at senior leader level in two secondary schools (one a large inner-city school, the other a small rural school) and have at one time or another managed every aspect of a school's organisation. I have managed the process of school improvement and self-evaluation, the curriculum and timetable, teaching and learning, pastoral care, administration, finance and the site. I have helped schools on the journey towards 'outstanding': one school became a beacon of good practice in teaching and learning; another became the highest achieving comprehensive school in its authority and one of the top five most improved schools in the country; a school judged 'good with outstanding features' under the new Ofsted framework within three years of emerging from 'special measures'. Along the journey, I've seen examples of good and bad leadership and have learnt valuable lessons from each. This book is a means of sharing those lessons in leadership.

The ABC of School Improvement covers a wide range of topics and for every chapter which explores the theory of effective school leadership, there's a series of practical resources and ideas which can be put to immediate use.

A caveat: no book can teach you how to be an effective school leader. What's more, there is no philosophy and no singular secret to share. The job of leading schools – as with leading any organisation – is far too complex and nuanced for that. To begin with, each leader is different: each leader has a personality and style of his or her own which is the culmination of unique life and work experiences. Each school and each student is different and requires a personalised approach. Each situation, too, is different and requires a pinch of pragmatism and common sense, plus a generous helping of humanity. In short: no problem is the same as the previous one and therefore no solution can be.

So the **ABC of School Improvement** cannot tell you how to deal with every situation you encounter but it can provide you with the tools you need to construct your own leadership style and build an outstanding school.

What is the ABC of School Improvement?

I've written this series around the notion that school improvement is as simple as ABC, where:

> **A** stands for *Assessment for Learning*,
> **B** stands for *Behaviour for Learning*, and
> **C** stands for *Curriculum for Learning*.

As well as a volume on each of these areas, I have added volumes on 'Leadership for Learning' and 'Future for Learning' in order to frame the school improvement process in context. In this volume, 'Leadership for Learning', I will explore what is meant by effective leadership and what school leaders need to do to drive the school improvement process forwards. In the final volume in the series, 'Future for Learning', I will explore the ever-changing educational landscape and consider the implications for schools of the latest government guidelines and policies.

Although I say that school improvement is as simple as ABC, I know a contrived mnemonic like this cannot begin to cover every aspect of a school's organisation. Moreover, I do not believe in simplifying every problem – schools are not simple places and their issues are complex and require complex thinking. Not everything can be reduced to its lowest common denominator. To be a successful school leader you need to wrestle with complexity and you need to know and understand the details. But once known and understood, you should try to frame them in a simple way and you should provide a means of communicating them so that they can be understood by others. Let me give you an example...

I have read – and indeed written – pages of text about the advantages and disadvantages of students starting GCSE courses in Year 9. Many schools are against it for very sound reasons, not least that students are more likely to achieve better grades in Year 11 than they are in Year 9 (because, in theory, students are more developed socially, emotionally and intellectually at 16 than they are at 14) and that students are already tested too much without adding to the burden in Year 9. I studied the arguments for and against and made my choice: I decided I wanted to offer a GCSE short course in Year 9 as a trial before considering whether to expand the practice, effectively creating a three-year Key Stage 4. And so I framed by argument, using my favoured 'list of three', as follows...

> Introducing a GCSE Short Course in Year 9 will:
> 1. **motivate** students with the early award of qualifications
> 2. allow us to **personalise** our curriculum
> 3. help **prepare** students for GCSE

I used these three words (motivate, personalise, prepare) throughout the documentation I produced on the subject – primarily for staff and governors – almost like a hypnotist manipulating his audience through the power of suggestion.

Behind each of these three statements was detailed analysis and data – but it was important for me to articulate my reasoning in a manner that would be clear and memorable. Reducing a complex argument to headlines like this is useful and effective in sharing your vision and winning support. Tony Blair was often accused of prioritising style over substance; he was supposedly obsessed with spin. But he was right to recognise the importance of 'message', of effective communication, in this technological age of 24/7 news and social media. Schools, like governments, need to control their message because parents and the community have more access to information than ever before and are more involved in the process of school improvement - not to mention school inspection.

So, I do not believe in simplifying complex issues – and acknowledge that school improvement is not as simple as ABC – but I do believe in simple communication, in simplifying your vision and your mission, in simplifying your message. I believe in simplifying what it is that your school stands for and what your school is trying to achieve. That way, it is more easily communicated and more easily understood. And if it is understood by all, it is shared more readily and realised more expediently.

This is why I believe this series of books, the ABC of School Improvement, is different and has a place, not on your bookshelves – gathering dust like the books on school leadership gather dust on my bookshelves – but on your desk, bookmarked and annotated with various marginalia: the way all good books should be.

How does the ABC of school improvement work in practice?

I believe in the importance of connectedness, in every cog in the machine working together in order to achieve something bigger and better than any single cog could produce on its own. In terms of school improvement, I believe that a school's vision should inform its improvement plan, which in turn should inform the process of performance management and continuing professional development (CPD). Whole-school targets should feed into faculty or departmental targets, which in turn should feed into individuals' targets. The whole school should be working together, pulling in the same direction.

The 'ABC of school improvement' can provide the framework your school needs in order to achieve **connectedness**:

Vision: the school's vision could be in three parts – a vision for assessment for learning; a vision for behaviour for learning, and a vision for curriculum for learning.

Targets: the school's targets could be informed by this vision: three targets or priorities for the year ahead, one for assessment, one for behaviour and one for curriculum.

Staffing structure: similarly, if these priorities are to be given weight and accountability, the senior team's structure could be hung on the concept of ABC whereby you have a senior leader responsible for assessment for learning, one responsible for behaviour for learning, and one for curriculum for learning.

School improvement plan: with this clear staffing structure in place, the school improvement plan should appear ready-formed; a section for each member of the SLT to lead, thereby increasing accountability and ensuring a clarity of purpose, a clear direction of travel.

Isn't this all just theory?

Even at this early stage, this book may well appear a little too theoretical – doing exactly what I said I wouldn't do: avoiding the practical – so allow me to put some meat on the bones. What do I actually mean – in practice – by my ABC: assessment for learning; behaviour for learning; and curriculum for learning?

The full contents page for this series will give you a good indication of what I mean by each of the three elements that make up the ABC of school improvement. For example, in the volume on Assessment for Learning I have written chapters about school improvement planning and self-evaluation, chapters about using data and target-setting, and chapters about lesson planning and intervention because each of these represent elements of what I term 'Assessment for Learning' (as distinct from Paul Black and Dylan Wiliam's seminal book of the same name). Using the chapters of this series as a guide, here is a breakdown of what specific, practical components of a school's organisation might make up the A, B and C:

ASSESSMENT FOR LEARNING

School improvement planning
Self-evaluation
Performance management
Data and target-setting
Assessment and reporting

BEHAVIOUR FOR LEARNING

Behaviour management
Rewards and sanctions
Vulnerable learners and differentiation
Student support and intervention
Every child matters & child protection

CURRICULUM FOR LEARNING

Curriculum design and development
Options and timetabling
Personalised learning pathways
Community cohesion and collaboration
Specialism

This is by no means an exhaustive list and the contents of this series will go into much more detail but I hope it provides a useful starting point or checklist. These lists may, for example, form part of senior leaders' roles and responsibilities (with the headteacher, business manager and finance manager taking up those elements covered by 'Volume One: Leadership for Learning') and may inform the three sections of your school improvement plan. For example, Section A of the plan may feature targets for improving the use of data and improving the process of target-setting across the school. Section B may feature targets for improving the quality of differentiation in lessons and for improving the systems of support in place for vulnerable students. Section C of the school improvement plan may contain targets for improving the physical environment, for providing more (or more appropriate) extra-curricular activities and for engaging with the community more effectively.

I will discuss the school improvement plan in more detail in Volume Two Chapter One (and will give you a sample school improvement plan to use); I will also expand on vision and mission in Volume One Chapter Two. But for now let's begin at the beginning... with **Volume One: Leadership for Learning**.

M J Bromley, March 2012

CHAPTER ONE:

Being a senior leader

What is school leadership?

School leadership – like all forms of leadership – is about setting direction. This is done by agreeing and articulating a shared vision, then by setting clear goals and performance targets that help bring that vision about.

The role of a school leader is often misunderstood and its scope underestimated by those outside the teaching profession. They remember the heads and deputy heads from their own childhoods as little more than the school's chief disciplinarians and the people who spoke soporifically in assemblies. But since the advent of grant-maintained status (following the Education Reform Act of 1988) school leaders have been much more than that: today, they are akin to the CEOs, finance directors and HR directors of medium-sized businesses all rolled into one (and this is not to mention their continuing role as chief disciplinarians and soporific speakers).

School leaders, therefore, have their fingers in many pies: they manage people; they manage projects; they manage processes; they manage information and communication; they manage finances, the site and health and safety; they develop and foster systems for monitoring, evaluating and reviewing performance; they manage governance; and they develop themselves and others - creating future leaders - using systems and processes wisely. This is a big job and if school leaders are to strike a healthy work-life balance (which they must if they are to survive their first term) they must not micro-manage each of these areas personally but must instead empower others - through artful delegation and through the creation of effective leadership structures - to be accountable.

Good school leaders, then, are about strategy and direction not day-to-day management. Good school leaders should concentrate on modelling the behaviours they expect from others (such as positivity and optimism, passion and determination). Good school leaders should develop people through support and understanding and should re-design their organisation (through a process of collaboration) in order to become - or continue to be - outstanding.

A good school leader is synonymous with being:
- ✓ a good listener; able to care about and respond to people's needs
- ✓ consistent, fair and honest; transparent and above reproach
- ✓ sensitive, able to show warmth and to empathise with people's concerns and worries
- ✓ able to give quality time to people, be available and approachable
- ✓ able to show assertiveness, determination and strength of response, yet be kind and calm and courageous
- ✓ able to communicate - through a variety of means and in an appropriate manner - with enthusiasm, passion and drive.

A good school leader should not and must not be consumed by what other people think. It is important that they are guided by their school's shared vision, and by their own determination and commitment to make a genuine and positive difference to young people's lives.

Moreover, a school's stakeholders - staff and governors, parents and students - will respond to a school leader who:
- ✓ is dynamic and forward thinking
- ✓ is sensitive to the needs of all and recognises hard work
- ✓ provides the necessary support others need
- ✓ trusts his/her staff and empowers them to make decisions and act on their own initiative
- ✓ does not place undue administrative burdens on his/her staff (i.e. keeps 'paper work' to a minimum and only calls meetings that serve a purpose)

What is the measure of a good school leader?

There are many ways to evaluate the effectiveness of a school leader but perhaps the most effective – and indeed ubiquitous – are the National Standards for Headteachers (sometimes referred to as the Six Key Areas). The standards were developed by the excellent National College for School Leadership (NCSL) and form part of the National Professional Qualification for Headship (NPQH) assessment criteria. Many schools have since adopted the Six Key Areas as their own measure of effective senior leadership (at all levels) and the standards also appear in job descriptions and person specifications, and are often the backbone of senior leader interviews.

The six key areas are:

1. Shaping the future
2. Leading teaching and learning
3. Developing self and working with others
4. Managing the organisation
5. Securing accountability
6. Strengthening community

Each school and each senior leader will have a different interpretation of what the standards mean to him or her in practice but here is my summary:

Shaping the future

Shaping the future is a key responsibility of any senior leader because, as I have discussed above and will explore in more detail in Chapter 2, senior leaders need to have a vision for their school and need to articulate this clearly and with enthusiasm to stakeholders. Senior leaders need to know what sort of organisation they want their school to be and this should guide their decision-making. Senior leaders should take account of their school's local and national context, not only in terms of their vision but also in their everyday actions. They should think strategically and involve their stakeholders in their decisions. They need to show conviction of purpose: they must be driven by their vision and not be distracted by setbacks or conflicts.

Leading teaching and learning

Schools are seats of learning and so leading the teaching and learning agenda is a key role of senior leaders. Leading teaching and learning is about having high expectations of all your teachers and about demanding the best for every learner in your school. This means leading by example by continuing to be an excellent classroom practitioner who is able to engage and enthuse students, and by being up-to-date with the latest pedagogical thinking. This also means evaluating teaching and learning effectively – through a variety of means including lesson observations, learning walks, student voice, work sampling and the scrutiny of assessment records – and working with others to improve the quality of teaching and learning (through professional learning communities and INSET, for example) and to challenge underachievement (by working with data and investing in intervention and support).

Developing self and working with others

Senior leaders need to foster a collaborative culture and provide learning opportunities for all their staff. They need to value the importance of continuing professional development (CPD) through performance management and INSET opportunities. They should have high expectations of everyone in their school. Senior leaders should, again, lead by example and take their own professional development seriously. They should be well-informed and up-to-date with the latest educational thinking and research, as well as government policy (central and local).

Managing the organisation

Senior leaders should share responsibility through effective delegation. They should demonstrate good judgment, be decisive but thoughtful, and should manage school resources effectively. They should manage their school's finances (although the day-to-day management of school finances should be delegated to a finance manager, this is one aspect of school leadership for which a headteacher should retain responsibility; a headteacher should fully understand the school finances and be accountable for fiscal decisions) in order to ensure their school achieves value for money. It is a senior leader's duty to use public money wisely. This is achieved by being prudent, by planning ahead (including detailed costs in the school improvement plan) and by prioritising spending according to greatest need and according to the impact that spending will have on learning (of which more in Chapter Six).

Senior leaders should also manage the site ensuring it complies with health and safety regulations and safeguarding. Senior leaders need to ensure that resources match the curriculum. Finally, senior leaders should manage the school's most important – and costly – resource: staff. This means ensuring that supply meets demand (in practice, this might involve restructuring) and that all staff have the tools and skills they need in order to do their jobs well (this means appropriate training but also evaluating whether staff have the requisite capability and, if not, taking appropriate action). Managing the organisation is often a part of the job that school leaders find most challenging and difficult because they have trained as teachers not managers, but it is also the most important part of the job if a school is to move forwards and achieve sustainable improvements.

Securing accountability

Senior leaders should take responsibility for their decisions and for the performance of their school. They should ensure clear accountability at all levels through effective line management structures and by drawing clear links between the school improvement plan and what is happening in school. They should analyse performance regularly and robustly, and give clear feedback and performance reports to stakeholders. Senior leaders have legal accountability for what happens in their school as well as moral accountability. They should do what they think is right and should take advice from others – including their local authority and trade unions – wherever possible. But above all they should do what is right for their school and take decisions that will stand up to tough scrutiny over the long-term.

Strengthening community

Senior leaders should develop and encourage effective partnerships with other schools, agencies and the community. Community cohesion is often misunderstood – or at least underestimated – as only referring to a school offering its site to the local community. Enabling community use is certainly important – be that by leasing your fields to the local football team or by running adult education classes in the evenings – but community cohesion is also about respecting diversity and protecting vulnerable learners. It is about understanding the local community and taking account of where students come from. It is about working with parents. It is about bringing the world into schools to raise students' awareness of the world. It is about responding to the Every Child Matters agenda (of which more in Volume Three Chapter Six) and respecting diversity and inclusion of all types, ensuring a personalised learning programme in which every child has the opportunity to fulfil his or her potential irrespective of socio-economic or ethnic background.

Work Life Balance

The qualities and skills listed above are all vital weapons in a senior leader's armoury but it is also important that leaders retain perspective and lead healthy lifestyles if they are to cope with the demands of the job and achieve longevity. The term 'work-life balance' is frequently used but, in my experience, rarely understood. Leaders accept that it is healthy to have a life outside of work but rarely acknowledge that this is also a sign of increased effectiveness. Too many people think that keeping sensible working hours is a sign of laziness or is symptomatic of a lack of commitment. Some people measure a leader's ability by how early his or her car pulls into the car park and by what time of night it drives away again. Nothing could be further from the truth.

The phrase 'work smarter not harder' may have become a hackneyed cliché but its sentiment remains as true today as it has always been. We all know colleagues who boast about the long hours they work. They tell us they've been in school since 6 o'clock that morning and didn't leave the office until 7 o'clock the previous night as if this is, in some way, a measure of ability or effectiveness. They wear their work ethic like a medal, proud to be so industrious. Like Boxer in George Orwell's 'Animal Farm' they find just one answer to every problem: 'I must work harder'. But let us take a quick walk through some of modern history's greatest achievements…

Every time there's been a significant and lasting improvement in the way we work (be that in terms of efficiency, revenue-generation or workers' conditions) it has been brought about, not by working harder, but by working smarter. The agricultural revolution, the industrial revolution and the technological revolution are perhaps the clearest examples of moments in history when the world of work has been, well, revolutionised for the better. And each revolution has been about inventing a way of working smarter: be that by developing better tools, by improving our knowledge and understanding, or by improving the quality of our communications.

For example, the increases in productivity and output brought about by the agricultural revolution were the result of advances in science, engineering and botany such as: enclosure, mechanisation, crop-rotation systems, and selective breeding. These were ways of working smarter; they did not result in farmers having to work longer hours – indeed, Jethro Tull's seed drill reduced the amount of labour required to plough and sow fields.

Equally, the industrial revolution – during which time income grew tenfold and the population grew sixfold – was about changes in technology and transport. It's true to say that the effects of the industrial revolution on working conditions were not immediate – it was not untypical for mill-workers to work 10 hours a day during the 19th century – but the invention of machines fuelled by water and steam gradually led to improved conditions. The concentration of labour in mechanised mills also improved the organisation of labour which allowed trade unions to fight for improved working conditions. Later, trains, ships, and the internal combustion engine improved trade which gave further momentum to economic progress.

The technological revolution – a phrase often used to describe a second wave of industrial revolution corresponding to the latter half of the 19th century but here used to describe the advancement of information and communications technology in the latter half of the 20th century and early part of the 21st century – has continued in this vein. The personal computer, the mobile 'phone, email, internet and social networking have all helped us to work smarter and, crucially, to work fewer hours. Communication is now instantaneous; we are able to share information more readily.

As a result of the agricultural revolution, the industrial revolution and the technological revolution we are able to work smarter not harder. And we need to learn the lessons of the last few hundred years and realise that effective organisation and appropriate delegation are signs of a successful, skilled leader; working twelve hours a day are not.

Working unsocial hours – depriving oneself of a life outside of work – is a measure of one's ineffectiveness. An effective school leader should be able to manage his or her time effectively and delegate appropriately in order to fulfil his or her duties within reasonable working hours. Organisation and delegation are basic management skills, after all. Moreover, an effective school leader should model a healthy work-life balance. An effective school leader should lead by example in showing his or her colleagues that it is important to have a life outside of work because doing so increases a person's sense of perspective and improves their quality of judgment. It helps to minimise stress. Enjoying a life outside of work adds to a person's life experiences and frame of reference. They can relate to colleagues and to students more readily if they experience life outside of school. At its simplest level, watching last night's episode of Coronation Street gives you a shared experience with colleagues and students – you have something with which to connect to other people. Spending time with family or friends, allowing the events of the day to melt away, allows you to distance yourself from those events and therefore to establish some perspective about their relative importance. That is not to say the events that seem of vital importance by day become irrelevant by night. As a school leader you deal with serious matters which require serious thought and care. But it is right that school leaders remain detached – emotionally speaking – and are able to make logical, strategic decisions which stand up to long-term scrutiny; not rash decisions of the heart, decisions taken under stress.

Let me make clear that being a school leader is not *just* a job: it is a career and something you should feel passionately about. It is important that school leaders do their jobs well. But that does not mean they should work all hours of day and night; nor does it mean they would be better at their jobs and get more done if they did so.

So, how do school leaders strike the right work-life balance? Everyone has a different way of working but being organised is clearly at the heart of it. There are various ways to organise your workload and I discuss many of them in this book. Here are just three examples to begin with:

- **Keep lists** – prioritise tasks according to their importance and timescale; make informed decisions about the relative impact of the actions that are asked of you upon students' learning and well-being. For example, use a 1 to 3 scale (or traffic lights) whereby 1 is urgent (usually to be completed within 24 hours), 2 is important (within 2 to 3 days) and 3 is neutral (ideally by the end of the week but often by the end of the month or half-term). There should be a fourth category: items to be delegated.

- **Delegate -** knowing which tasks can be delegated and to whom is important; keeping track of those tasks – striking the right balance between giving colleagues genuine ownership of the task and ensuring it is completed on time – is also important.

- **Keep meetings short and productive** – this can be done by circulating a clear, agreed agenda prior to the meeting and doggedly sticking to that agenda, ensuring that deviations are avoided. The minutes of meetings (which I will explore in more detail later) should be short and should list the actions required and the people responsible for their completion. Meetings are often important, unavoidable and the most effective way of making decisions. But knowing when a meeting is necessary and when meetings can be avoided is just as important. Ask yourself: can I achieve the same outcome without a meeting? Can the matter be resolved by email, a telephone call or a 'walk and talk'? If a meeting is necessary, what is the best format? A formal, round the table meeting or a short, standing briefing?

Colleagues will respond better to meetings if they know they are only held when necessary.

What do school leaders need to do in order to aid improvement?

This series is called the 'ABC of School Improvement' so let us now focus on how senior leaders – whilst displaying the qualities and skills discussed above – can help bring about school improvement.

Firstly, it is the responsibility of school leaders to create effective structures in which:
> there is a clear vision of what is trying to be achieved
> targets are realistic and achievable
> true delegation is offered and senior staff are empowered to make decisions
> effective communication systems are in place;
> purposeful meetings are called; meetings are minuted and actions set
> paper work is kept to a minimum
> all staff know exactly who does what
> actions are delivered within the context of the school improvement plan
> students are at the centre of any decisions and changes
> there are effective monitoring and evaluative procedures in place at all levels
> there is clear value for money in terms of the school's effectiveness and efficiency.

We will examine each of these conditions during the course of this series, starting with the **vision**.

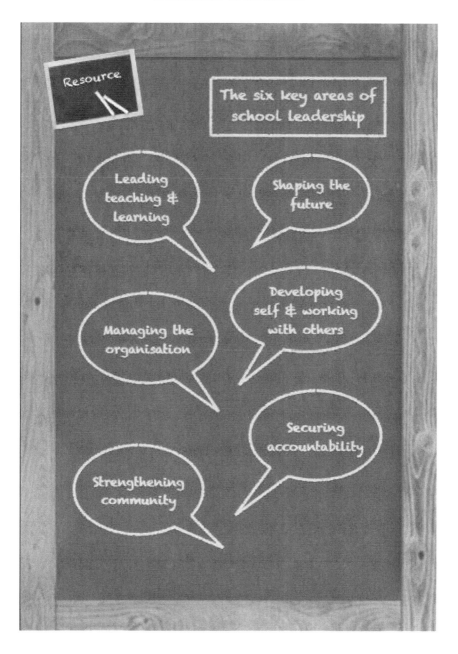

M J BROMLEY

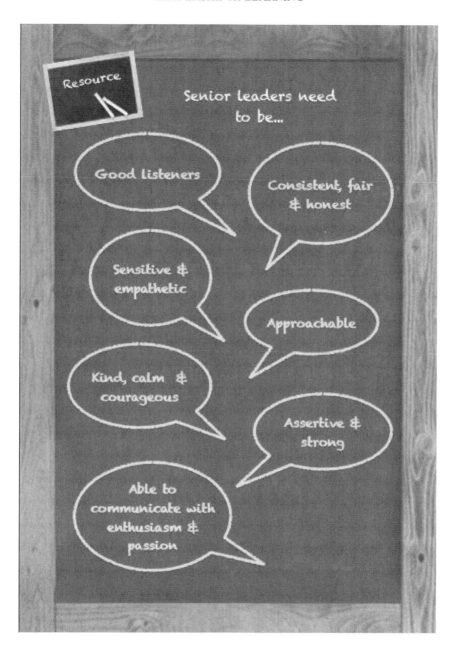

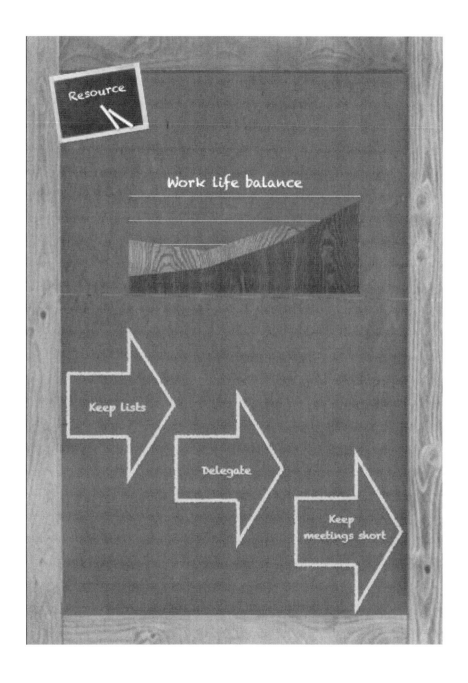

CHAPTER TWO

Vision and mission

What's the difference between a vision statement and a mission statement?

I find it useful to think of the two terms, which are often used interchangeably, in the following way: vision is your destination; mission is your means of transport.

In other words, a vision statement sets out what you want your school to be like whereas a mission statement articulates the behaviours and values, systems and processes, you expect your school to adopt in order to get there.

What makes a good vision statement?

Firstly, a school's vision should be shared. It is all well and good for the headteacher to have a clear vision of what he or she wants to achieve but it will remain an aspiration and will never be achieved if it is not understood and shared by everyone else in the organisation. The vision will only be realised if every classroom teacher, every teaching assistant, every member of support staff and every middle and senior leader makes it happen through their everyday behaviours and actions. It is no use having a vision which many staff disagree with or misunderstand, or which does not suit the school's context. It has to make sense, be achievable and be meaningful. It has to take the school forward in the right direction. It has to be something everyone wants to see take shape. In other words, it has to benefit everyone. Ideally, it should express what is unique about the school not be an 'off-the-peg' statement which could easily be applied to any school in any part of the country.

A good starting point when writing your vision statement is your school's existing vision. If it does not have one, then your school's motto is a helpful place to begin. Why? Because although the vision statement is about the future, it should also have solid foundations in the past, in the school's history, in what the school stands for and why it exists. Continuity is important to all those with a stake in the school. No one likes change, it is uncomfortable. People like to know that what they have built, what they have worked hard for, is to be retained and protected. A vision which refers to what the school already does well *and* articulates what it hopes to do better in the future keeps everyone happy. Moreover, it is balanced, fair and, above all, cohesive: it binds stakeholders together.

On the subject of cohesion, all staff and governors need to be involved in agreeing the vision but this does not have to mean a long and convoluted process of wrangling over every word. Instead, the senior team - or perhaps a working party representing as many different areas of staff as possible - should draft a vision for wider consultation. That consultation should be clearly framed: what do you want to consult on, what are the dividing lines? Make it clear what is open for debate and what is not. Do you want to debate every word or do you want to debate broad principles? Make clear what form you expect the consultation to take and how you will garner feedback. Make clear how you will respond to that feedback. People need to feel listened to but you do not want to promise something you cannot deliver.

As well as the school's motto, the vision should be informed by the school's current (3-year) priorities or targets which in turn are likely to be informed by the latest Ofsted report, the latest data analysis and 3-year trend data, and a review of the latest school improvement plan. As discussed in the Introduction to this book, the vision could well be three-pronged with a vision for assessment for learning, a vision for behaviour for learning and a vision for curriculum for learning. That way the vision bleeds into the school improvement plan and staffing structure, ensuring clear lines of accountability and a clear message about what the school hopes to achieve, how it intends to achieve it and who is responsible for making it happen.

As a starting point – using the kind of statements associated with 'outstanding' schools, you might like to consider the following:

> Our school is committed to the pursuit of excellence, values people, delivers achievements for all, provides a high-quality learning environment, and extends the boundaries of learning. Learning is personalised and engaging; it enables all students to achieve his/her full potential and provides every young person with a gateway to future success.

I must stress that this vision is provided as a template. It should be personalised to your school's context and should be more specific (less bland) about what your school wants to achieve in the medium-term (2 to 3 years).

What makes a good mission statement?

The mission statement is necessarily longer than the vision statement. It is a detailed declaration of what your school will do in order to achieve its vision. It should try to cover all the important aspects of a school's working practices. It should, for example, cover: how it uses data; what kind of curriculum it has or aspires to have; what the atmosphere should be like; how it caters for vulnerable learners; how it engages with the local community; and so on.

Again as a starting point, you may wish to consider the following mission statement:

> Our school is a place where:
> - there is a shared vision of what the school is trying to achieve;
> - data is understood and acted upon appropriately;
> - students make good or better progress within each year and key stage, academically, emotionally and socially;
> - there is a rich curriculum taught by skilled, well-motivated teachers;
> - there is a purposeful, organised working atmosphere, students are valued and their contributions are appreciated;
> - resources, including quality ICT provision, are well-matched to the curriculum;
> - students are challenged and encouraged to do their best;
> - vulnerable children are identified early and support mechanisms are put in place;
> - parents are fully informed and are welcomed contributors to school life;
> - there is a sense of involvement in the local community and visitors and outside agencies provide contributions to the school;
> - all staff are valued and are supported in their own personal and professional development;
> - standards reflect the status of the students: there is no coasting, and realistic achievement targets are consistently met;
> - the school is held in high esteem by the local community;
> - there is appropriate and interesting extra-curricular provision.

What should you do with the vision and mission once written and ratified?

Once the vision statement and mission statement have been agreed, they need to be officially ratified by governors. Once ratified, they should not be filed away in a dusty drawer and forgotten about. They should be placed centre-stage. They should be referred to as frequently as possible and should underpin everything the school does.

In practice, this might mean:

➤ Including the vision statement on letter-headed paper, in the school prospectus and newsletters

➤ Using the vision to frame the school's 3-year targets or priorities

➤ Including the vision and mission on the front page of the school improvement plan and using it to frame the plan: a section of the plan for each aspect of the vision, broken down into specific actions that will help to realise the vision

➤ Including the vision and mission on the front page of the self-evaluation form (SEF)

➤ Including the vision and mission in faculty or departmental action plans

➤ Including the vision in performance management documentation and using the vision to provide a broad basis for all staff's targets

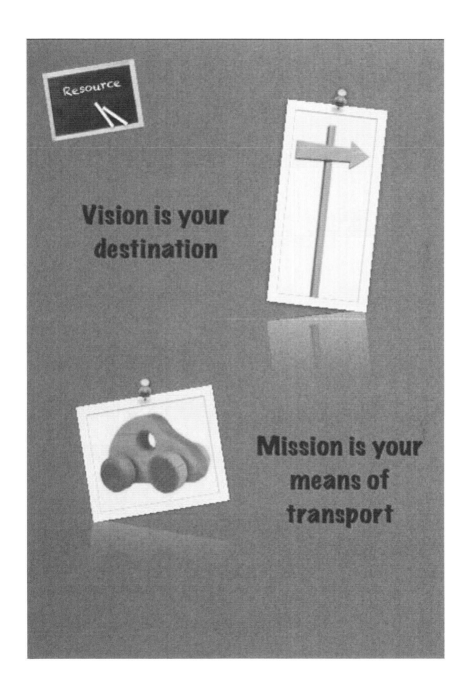

CHAPTER THREE

Becoming outstanding

Leaders not managers...

Schools need leaders not managers to oversee the process of school improvement.

Leadership and management are words often glued together like 'salt and pepper' and 'knife and fork' but they are actually quite different. Yes, it is true that most leaders are appointed because they have a proven track record as good managers; and, yes, it is true that good leaders need to continue practising their management skills. But nevertheless the two are different. Whereas managers bring order and organisation; leaders bring change and challenges. Managers are concerned with the short-term; leaders with the long-term. Managers solve problems and achieve goals; leaders pose questions and generate options and opportunities.

Put simply:
- **managers are operational**
- **leaders are strategic**.

I introduced two types of SLT meeting at my last school: SLT 'strategy' meetings which took place after school as part of the whole-school meeting cycle (about once every three weeks) and SLT 'operational' meetings which took place within the school day (and once a week). The agenda for these meetings were distinct: strategy meetings were concerned with long-term planning and were focused on discussions around the school improvement plan – where we are and where we're going (and often resulted in updates to the SEF); operational meetings were concerned with the here and now, with what had happened over the previous week and what was coming up in the next week. Strategy meetings were about vision and mission, creating a long-term plan and articulating what we aspired to achieve in the future; operational meetings were about the day-to-day running of a school, solving yesterday's problems for tomorrow. In other words, strategy meetings were about leadership; operational meetings were about management. I found the distinction helpful.

Managers need a range of skills including: communication, organisation, operational leadership, managing difficult staff and managing difficult situations.

Leaders need **strategic vision** (to be able to see clearly where they and their school are going, to be able to aim high and share their passion and determination with others, to be able to communicate their plans with enthusiasm and clarity) and **strategic planning** (knowing where their school is now, where they want to go and how they're going to get there).

As I say above, schools need effective senior leaders to drive school improvement. They must distribute leadership and empower others to make decisions, they must not micro-manage every goal and target on the school improvement plan. They need oversight, they need to be able to see the 'bigger picture' and draw various elements together. They do not need to know all the details, just be reassured that someone else does.

Two starting principles of school improvement...

Talk isn't cheap...

Leaders of school improvement must talk to their staff – communication is the key to success. Staff must feel informed and involved in the process of improvement. Leaders should be open and honest with colleagues and should seek to reach agreement where possible but should not be afraid to make difficult – perhaps unpopular – decisions when this is right for the school. Leaders must not abdicate responsibility but should share it. Where a decision is taken which is not consensual, the rationale should be clearly explained and staff should understand the benefits of that decision for the school and its students. Leaders should not see it as a weakness to ask for help or advice from colleagues or others; nor should they be afraid to admit when they get it wrong. It is a strength, not a weakness, to be self-aware and pragmatic, to adapt to changing circumstances and respond to evolving situations.

Tweak not transform...

Change is uncomfortable and unsettling. People are not at their best when experiencing change. Not only should leaders be open and honest about the changes that are needed; not only should they communicate the rationale behind change and outline the benefits of change; they should also try to avoid unnecessary change. It is important to understand the status quo, to know what works well and what should be protected and retained. It is important to identify the foundations on which to build. People do not like change because it is uncomfortable and challenging. People like to know their hard work has purpose and meaning. Change needs to be incremental; the future needs to be built on the foundations of the past.

What does an outstanding school look like?

Put simply, an outstanding school is a school which has all the following components...

1 *Effective leadership:* an outstanding school needs effective leadership, leadership which is strong and has a clear direction, leadership which is inclusive of all staff and students.

2 *A shared vision:* an outstanding school needs a shared vision, a clear idea of where it is headed (a common goal) and how it is going to get there; an outstanding school also needs an effective school improvement plan and effective systems of monitoring and evaluating performance which are understood by all staff.

3 *Data is understood and action is taken:* an outstanding school is one in which data is understood by all staff and in which data is used to drive improvements, to aid progress and to avoid underachievement.

4 *Students make progress:* an outstanding school is one in which students make good or better progress, where students are given aspirational targets and where intervention is early and effective and personalised, where student progress is tracked and students are rewarded for hard work.

5 *A rich curriculum:* an outstanding school is one in which there is a broad, engaging curriculum which meets the needs of all students and provides a gateway to future success.

6 *Staff are supported and motivated:* an outstanding school is one in which staff are well-supported and cared for, and where they are motivated to work hard and take pride in a job well done. An outstanding school is one in which professional development is taken seriously and staff are valued and have the tools they need to do their jobs.

7 *Purposeful environment:* an outstanding school is one in which there is a well-organised and attractive environment – an environment which is physically engaging and conducive to learning; as well as metaphysically engaging with effective (i.e. not bureaucratic and not time-consuming) systems and structures.

8 *Vulnerable students are identified and supported:* an outstanding school is one in which vulnerable children are identified, their needs are known and in which staff are appropriately trained and have the skills to support them effectively.

9 *Students are challenged and encouraged:* an outstanding school is one in which students are challenged and encouraged to work hard and are rewarded for their efforts, where students are engaged in their learning but where there are also clear, effective sanctions in place.

10 *Parents and the community are informed and contribute:* an outstanding school is one in which parents have a voice and can contribute to school life, and where the community and the school work together for the benefit of all. An outstanding school is one in which governors take an active interest in school life, are knowledgeable about what happens in school, and strike the right balance between support and challenge: they are a critical friend working as servants of the school - indeed, acting as ambassadors of the school in the wider community - but are not afraid to question its direction.

11 *A range of extra-curricular activities:* an outstanding school is one in which there are a variety of engaging and appropriate extra-curricular activities which extend the boundaries of learning and provide a safe environment for young people. An outstanding school also provides extra-curricular activities which actively encourage community involvement and participation, and widen students' knowledge and experience.

CHAPTER FOUR

Managing change

Any process of school improvement necessarily involves change because, if a school is to improve, it must change. Managing change, therefore, is an important skill for school leaders. Many senior leaders enjoy working against a backdrop of continuous change because it makes their jobs interesting, challenging and varied. It gives them a chance to stamp their mark on the organisation, to show what they are capable of. But it's important to remember that not everyone shares this passion for change.

Leaders should start with the knowledge that change can be uncomfortable, particularly for those who feel that change is being done *to* them not *by* them. Leaders should also bear in mind that many staff will resent change and will either refuse to engage with it or, worse, act to prevent it from happening. And, as I say above, a school can only become outstanding if everyone works together. So what is the best way to manage change? First, it is important to understand why people are resistant to it...

People are resistant to change because:
- They are anxious of the impact it will have on their jobs
- They feel they have tried it before and it didn't work
- They fear it will mean more work for them
- They do not understand the need for change, they like the status quo
- They fear failure
- They are scared by the pace of change and by being out of their comfort zone
- They fear change will prove too costly or a waste of time and money

People are resistant to change because change implies that the status quo isn't good enough, that the way people work now is in some way inadequate. People also resent change because it signals the destruction of all they have worked hard to achieve. Change means abandoning what they know and what they like. All of these things may be true, of course: the status quo may not be good enough; the way people work now may indeed be inadequate. But it is unlikely your school is so thoroughly broken that it requires a total transformation. It is more likely that there will be lots of things about your school that should be retained, preserved, protected. Even if it is so utterly broken that it needs wholesale change, the process of mending it should be done gradually and with the support of staff: this means careful management, a lot of tact and patience.

Once you understand people's resistance to change, you should begin to engage them in the process of change. As a starting point, it is important to:

- Be **open and honest** about the need for change: involve your staff as early as possible, ideally involve them in the process of identifying the need for change in the first place.

- Explain the **rationale behind change**: on what evidence have you based your decision to change? What do you hope this change will achieve and why is that important?

- Outline the **benefits of change** for everyone: what is it in for staff, students, parents and governors? How will change make their working lives easier and more rewarding?

Senior leaders need to use the following skills when managing change:

Patience and self-control:
Staying calm and considered, being rational

Balance:
Balancing the needs of students with the needs of staff, balancing the need to improve teaching and learning with the school's financial needs

Communication:
Keeping others informed and involved

Problem-solving:
Thinking through the options, finding appropriate solutions

Personal ownership:
Showing initiative and being conscientious, taking responsibility

Leaders of change also need enthusiasm, flexibility, energy and tenacity if they are to succeed in bringing about lasting, positive change which leads to genuine and sustainable school improvement.

I find a change management cycle useful in planning for change. I share an example of a change management cycle I have used to good effect at the end of this chapter. I'd like to cite the now defunct Training and Development Agency (TDA) for helping me formulate this and some of the other ideas that follow. Their 'Little Book of Change' [2008] is an excellent resource and contains a lot of useful change management tools.

The cycle I use revolves as follows:
1. **Mobilise**
2. **Discover**
3. **Deepen**
4. **Develop**
5. **Deliver**

What does the change management cycle mean in practice?

Mobilise

First, it is important to understand why some colleagues may resist change. You need to tackle this head-on by explaining why change is necessary (where is the need, what is the rationale?) and by outlining the benefits of change for everyone involved. Then you need to involve your staff in the process of change: don't let them see change as something being done to them by the senior team, let them feel genuinely a part of the process and able to contribute to it and affect it. A good way to mobilise staff is to establish **'change teams'** or working parties which will be the driving force behind change. Change teams should be representative of all staff.

Discover

One of the first jobs for the change team is to identify and acknowledge **the issues** involved in change. It means developing a deeper understanding of what change will involve and how barriers will be overcome. This might involve members of the change team consulting with others and bringing ideas and issues back to the table. For example, your change team may include a member of each department or faculty, a member of support staff and a teaching assistant. It may include a member of the admin team and/or site staff. Discovering the issues may be as simple as conducting a SWOT analysis or may be more complex.

Deepen

The change team then needs to develop a deeper knowledge and understanding of the *scale* and *scope* of the changes that are required. They also need to know and understand the root causes of the issues that led to change being needed in the first place, as well as the issues that will inevitably arise whilst change is being enacted. This stage is about being forewarned and forearmed, about being prepared for the road ahead. It is also about setting the boundaries - knowing what will be included in the project and what will not - and setting appropriate timescales.

Develop

This stage is about **suggesting solutions**, coming up with improvements to the way people work. It is about the change team taking action, trialling new methods of working and finding out what is effective and what isn't. It is important at this stage to prioritise those actions which will have the biggest impact. Start with a splash not a ripple. You want other staff to see the impact of what you're doing, you want them to see that change is for the better, that you are getting results *and* making life easier. You want to win over your detractors and those most resistant to change, you want to convince them that what you're doing is right. For example, your change team may trial a new teaching method - let's say the use of group work - and this may be videoed and played at a faculty meeting or on a training day in order to show all your staff that such an approach works in your school. This may then encourage others to try it out, too.

Deliver

This stage is about **making change happen**. The change team now rolls out the changes they have developed and refined to the whole school. The plans formed in the 'develop' stage are now fully agreed and everyone begins to implement them, again starting with the high impact actions or 'quick wins'.

In summary, effective change requires:

1. **Effective leadership** – leadership which is democratic, which acts as a role model, which supports and encourages others. Why? Because effective leadership leads to people feeling involved and valued, provides broader, richer insights and ideas, and helps improve staff morale, as well as recruitment and retention; effective leadership also shares responsibility, leads to less stress, higher standards of teaching, effective collaboration and more honest relationships in which problems are aired and resolved faster.

2. **Inclusive culture** – a culture in which people know they can contribute and overcome barriers together, in which everyone is encouraged to play a part in driving the school's change agenda.

3. **Broad collaboration** – collaboration between schools, stakeholders and other organisations which helps embed a culture of openness to positive change.

4. **Change teams** – working parties which are inclusive and representative of all areas of school, a team which acts as a communication channel between the senior team and the workforce and which makes staff feel involved in their school.

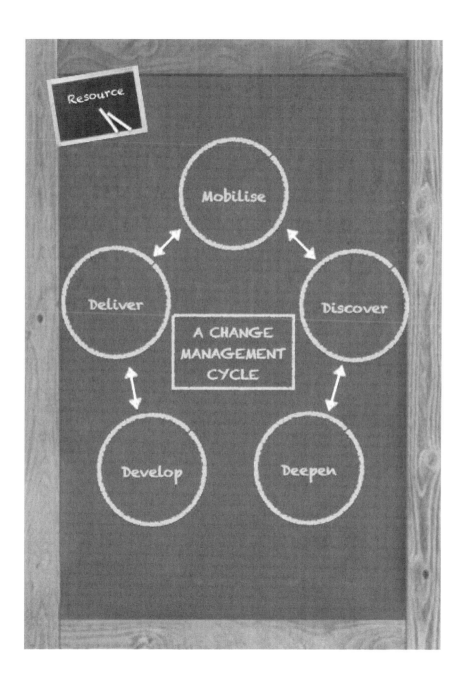

CHAPTER FIVE

Coaching and mentoring

A train travels along tracks and cannot deviate from its set route; a coach, by contrast, is able to travel in any direction and go wherever its passengers need it to. Equally, a trainer is someone who follows a set course (hence the term 'training course'); a trainer imparts knowledge in a set order. A coach, however, is someone who can allow him or herself to be led in new and interesting directions, to take detours, in order that the colleague they are coaching is afforded the opportunity to explore the issues that matter most to him or her, and in order to allow that person to find his or her own solution - to arrive at his or her own destination, if you will.

The purpose of coaching is to bring out the best in people by helping them to unlock their potential. Coaching is about teasing out answers from the person being coached through questioning and through challenging their perceptions and understanding. Coaching is about getting the person being coached (the coachee) to explore a situation they've recently experienced (or a situation they are about to experience) from a range of different angles and perspectives so that they might learn from those experiences and so that they might find their own solutions. A coach does not need to know more about a situation than the person being coached; indeed, no expert knowledge is needed and the best coaches are often peers.

I am indebted to the National College of School Leadership for helping me develop some of the ideas I explore in this chapter. I recommend their publication, 'Leading Coaching in Schools' [2005], to anyone wishing to know more on the subject.

What is the difference between coaching and mentoring?

In its report, 'Coaching for Teaching and Learning', the CfBT Education Trust says:

> In some contexts coaching and mentoring are used almost as interchangeable terms. Without doubt they are both valuable processes. It is true that the boundary between them is somewhat permeable and that often the same individuals in schools carry out or participate in both processes. But the CUREE framework distinguishes between three related processes as follows:
>
> 1. Mentoring is a structured, sustained process for supporting professional learners through significant career transitions.
> 2. Specialist coaching is a structured, sustained process for enabling the development of a specific aspect of a professional learner's practice.
> 3. Collaborative (Co-) coaching is a structured, sustained process between two or more professional learners to enable them to embed new knowledge and skills from specialist sources in day-to-day practice.

The CfBT also provide this useful comparison:

Coaching:
- Coaching is usually focused professional dialogue designed to aid the coachee in developing specific skills to enhance their teaching repertoire
- For teachers it often supports experimentation with new classroom strategies
- Coaches are not normally in positions of line management in relation to their coachee
- Coaching for enhancing teaching and learning is not normally explicitly linked to a career transition
- The focus of the coaching is usually selected by the coachee and the process provides opportunities for reflection and problem solving for both coach and coachee

Mentoring:
- Mentoring usually takes place at significant career events, such as to support induction or taking on new professional roles
- It has an element of 'gatekeeping' and the mentor is almost always someone more senior in the organisation
- There is often an organisational motive for the process; for example succession planning

➤ In some cases there is a requirement that the mentor provides documentary evidence of the mentoring process and its outcomes; for example demonstrating that the participant in mentoring has met certain competences

What is coaching?

Coaching takes many forms: from life coaching to executive coaching – and the aims, purposes and practices can be quite different. So what does all coaching have in common? And what are the general principles of coaching? A study conducted by CUREE in 2005 (which led to the National Framework for Mentoring and Coaching) concluded that:

- The focus of coaching is the in-depth development of specific knowledge, skills and strategies.

- Coaching does not depend on the coach having more experience than the coachee; it can take place between peers and staff at different levels of status and experience.

- Coaching is usually informed by evidence.

- Whilst mentoring can incorporate coaching activity, it tends to focus upon the individual's professional role, often as they move into new roles and take new responsibilities.

- A mentor is usually a more experienced colleague; someone very familiar with a particular culture and role, who has influence and can use their experience to help an individual analyse their situation in order to facilitate professional and career development.

CUREE lists Ten Principles of Coaching in its National Framework:

1. *A learning conversation:* structured professional dialogue, rooted in evidence from the professional learner's practice, which articulates existing beliefs and practices to enable reflection on them.

2. *Setting challenging and personal goals:* identifying goals that build on what learners know and can do already, but could not yet achieve alone, whilst attending to both school and individual priorities.

3. *A thoughtful relationship:* developing trust, attending respectfully and with sensitivity to the powerful emotions involved in deep professional learning.

4. Understanding why different approaches work: developing understanding of the theory that underpins new practice so it can be interpreted and adapted for different contexts.

5. A learning agreement: establishing confidence about the boundaries of the relationship by agreeing and upholding ground rules that address imbalances in power and accountability.

6. Acknowledging the benefits to the mentors and coaches: recognising and making use of the professional learning that mentors and coaches gain from the opportunity to mentor or coach.

7. Combining support from fellow professional learners and specialists: collaborating with colleagues to sustain commitment to learning and relate new approaches to everyday practice; seeking out specialist expertise to extend skills and knowledge and to model good practice.

8. Experimenting and observing: creating a learning environment that supports risk-taking and innovation and encourages professional learners to seek out direct evidence from practice.

9. Growing self-direction: an evolving process in which the learner takes increasing responsibility for their professional development as skills, knowledge and self-awareness increase.

10. Using resources effectively: making and using time and other resources creatively to protect and sustain learning, action and reflection on a day-to-day basis.

Effective coaching is dependent on the coachee being open and honest with the coach. The coachee needs to be willing to put the plans they make during their coaching session into practice. Accordingly, the National Framework sets out requirements for coachees as well as coaches. Those being coached, the framework says, need to: understand their own learning needs; reflect on their own practice; take an increasingly active role in their own learning; act on what is learned to improve pupil learning.

The National Framework states that coaching is grounded in five key skills:
1. establishing rapport and trust
2. listening for meaning
3. questioning for understanding
4. prompting action, reflection and learning
5. developing confidence and celebrating success

Therefore, a coach must: establish high levels of trust; be consistent over time; offer genuine respect; be honest, frank and open; and challenge without threat.

A coach must not: give answers or advice; make judgements; offer counselling; create dependency; impose agendas or initiatives; and confirm long-held prejudice.

What is mentoring?

Mentoring is about leading by example and offering solutions. The mentoring process is focused on developing a person within their professional role - perhaps, for example, helping them to progress within an organisation by stepping a rung up the career ladder. A mentor usually has more experience and knowledge than the mentee - he or she has been there and done that - and the mentor uses his or her own experiences in order to analyse the mentee's situation and offer help and advice on how to deal with it.

The National College of School Leaders defines mentoring in the following terms:

"It's a partnership between a less experienced mentee and the mentor, who uses their extensive professional experience of the mentee's role to help them develop a confident approach to the job. Mentoring is support aimed at professionals in a transition phase in their career, such as moving into the headteacher role.

"Mentors focus on listening and questioning rather than directing the mentee. Their aim is to help the mentee question their practice and come to their own conclusions about steps they may need to take to change or develop their approach to the job.

"It differs from coaching, which is less role-specific and is used for individuals who have been in a post for some time and feel confident in their position and understand the organisation".

Mentoring, like coaching, needs to be structured – quality time must be carved out for the mentoring session to take place and adequate time must also be allocated for preparation and reflection. Mentoring should not be seen as superfluous or somehow peripheral to the real work of a school; it should be integral and planned for. Mentoring sessions should be flexible, allowing for tangential talk, but they should also take place within an agreed, planned framework. Therefore, the mentor needs to plan the mentoring sessions carefully and should evaluate them afterwards.

Effective mentoring takes place when both the mentor and the mentee have thought about the past, present and future: they should analyse what has already happened in order to learn from it, they should consider what is happening right now in order to help shape it, and they should consider what needs to happen in the future in order to plan for it. As mentoring relies on the mentor's prior experience, mentors should be prepared to discuss their experiences, too, and explore what they did when faced with a similar situation, as well as what they learned from it. Unlike a coach, a mentor cannot be passive: they must be active and they must be open and honest.

Furlong and Maynard's 1995 study into the development of a trainee teacher is a useful diversion here because it informs us how new school staff undergo a common process of development: a process which can inform the act of mentoring. The stages are as follows:

Stage 1: early idealism – student teachers see their role as something that just happens without a great deal of effort on their part...

Stage 2: personal survival – student teachers are reactive rather than proactive, doing what is necessary to survive...

Stage 3: dealing with difficulties – student teachers replicate what they believe to be teacherly behaviour...

Stage 4: hitting a plateau – student teachers begin to gain confidence in their abilities but they *act* like a teacher rather than *think* like a teacher...

Stage 5: moving on – student teachers move on to understand the roles and responsibilities of a teacher.

[*adapted from* Furlong and Maynard, 1995]

Although I would define the stages of a student teacher's development in slightly different terms, this study is useful because it helps to think in terms of 'common' experiences like this when considering the mentoring process. Why? Because mentoring is likely to follow similar stages of development as the mentee expands his or her experiences, skills and knowledge.

Each mentoring session will be different because they will adapt as the mentee passes through each stage of his/her development. It is likely, too, that the emphasis will pass from the mentor to the mentee as the sessions proceed. The balance of support and challenge will also shift as time moves on. But, broadly speaking, each mentor session will be in three parts:

1. Past (or 'feedback'): setting out and agreeing the objectives for the session; dealing with the issues that have arisen since the last mentoring session, reviewing progress against the targets that were set at the last session or reviewing the mentee's recent experiences.

2. Present (or 'shaping'): discussing situations the mentee is currently involved in and situations which are enfolding presently; debating how he or she has dealt with the situation so far and how he or she intends to deal with the situation next, what he or she intends to do next.

3. Future (or 'planning'): learning from past and present experiences and allowing them to redefine the mentee in terms of their knowledge, skills and experience; stepping back and reflecting on how the mentee has developed and grown, and discussing how he or she will apply this learning to future situations; predicting and planning for future events.

What are the benefits of coaching and mentoring in schools?

The benefits of coaching and mentoring for the individuals being supported are perhaps obvious: they will become more motivated and their confidence will grow; their knowledge and skills will be enhanced and their experience will be enlarged – because they will learn more about themselves and more about their jobs as a result of the process.

But coaching and mentoring also benefit the organisation: staff who are motivated and confident in their work will show greater degrees of loyalty towards their school. This, in turn, will improve levels of recruitment and retention and aid the development of sustainable leadership – in other words, schools can grow their own leaders. But coaching and mentoring can also foster effective and genuine sharing between colleagues, as well as between departments and faculties. Sharing best practice helps to reduce inconsistencies and helps improve performance across the school.

Coaching and mentoring can be used to help school staff deal with a variety of situations including:

➢ managing student behaviour
➢ increasing student performance
➢ developing and fostering team spirit and effective team working
➢ developing staff who are new to their roles and responsibilities
➢ helping staff with career development
➢ improving teachers' performance and avoiding capability proceedings or disciplinaries
➢ developing lesson planning practices and improving teaching and learning
➢ developing marking and assessment practices
➢ supporting colleagues on ITT and GTP programmes, as well as NQTs

However, coaching and mentoring will only be effective in these situations if the school invests in them and takes them seriously. Coaching and mentoring need to be a part of a school's everyday working practices. There need to be appropriate structures and systems in place which encourage coaching and mentoring and which ensure it is a long-term solution. If this is so, coaching and mentoring will reap longer-term benefits.

In practice, this means investing time and money into coaching and mentoring and creating links with other organisations and networks. For example, coaching and mentoring should be linked to performance management. Coaching and mentoring should also be linked to the school improvement plan: developing coaching and mentoring can be an objective in its own right and the act of coaching and mentoring can be listed as a resource to bring about the completion of other objectives in the plan.

Coaching and mentoring should also be a part of the school's planned programme of CPD, perhaps even a whole-school INSET event because staff may need training before being coached/mentored or indeed before becoming a coach or mentor. This training may be around the notion of 'contracting': of agreeing the terms of the coaching/mentoring sessions and agreeing the intended outcomes; or it may be around the skills needed to question and challenge, to persevere and press for firm commitments.

Coaching and performance management might be linked in the following ways:

1. Coaching might be used by managers to address concerns raised through performance management
2. Evidence emerging from coaching might be used to inform the coachee's own performance management
3. Participants might elect to use coaching as a means of addressing an area of development identified through performance management

The future of coaching and mentoring in schools

Coaching and mentoring are becoming ever more integral to the way schools operate thanks to the introduction of 'teaching schools'. Schools - not universities or colleges – are becoming *the* places for training new teachers: more and more students are applying for graduate teaching posts rather than PGCE courses, and more and more schools are taking on the responsibility for training their own teachers rather than accommodating ITT students from other providers.

The concept of 'teaching schools' was introduced in 2011 in the coalition government's 'Importance of Teaching' white paper and is based on the existing model of teaching hospitals. The basic principle is that teaching schools will build on existing school-based initial teaching training programmes and existing continuing professional development programmes. The difference is that teaching schools will also:

- train new entrants to the profession by working with other partners such as universities

- lead peer-learning and professional development programmes, including the designation and deployment of specialist leaders of education (SLEs)

- identify and nurture leadership potential

- lead a local network of schools and other partners in order to improve the quality of teaching and learning

- help form a national network of schools to support them with innovation and the transfer of knowledge

- be at the heart of a new school improvement strategy or system that puts responsibility on the profession and on schools rather than on local authorities or the government

In his paper on the subject of teaching schools, David Hargreaves argues that, "It will not be enough for teaching schools to continue [with the traditional model] of professional development. Their challenging task is to raise professional development to a new level through the exemplary use and dissemination of joint practice development [which] "captures a process that is truly collaborative, not one-way; the practice is being improved, not just moved from one person or place to another":

Joint practice development gives birth to innovation and grounds it in the routines of what teachers naturally do. Innovation is fused with and grows out of practice, and when the new practice is demonstrably superior, escape from the poorer practice is expedited.

If joint practice development replaced sharing good practice in the professional vocabulary of teachers, we would, I believe, see much more effective practice transfer in the spirit of innovation that is at the heart of a self-improving system.

"Mentoring and coaching between schools," Hargreaves argues, "are at the heart of this effective practice transfer. A school that has not developed a strong mentoring and coaching culture is not likely to be successful either at moving professional knowledge and skills to partners or at rising to the level of joint practice development." He says effective use of coaching and mentoring is a means of nurturing talent and is of particular importance in leadership development "since leaders learn best with and from outstanding leaders."

He argues that effective mentoring and coaching in schools is defined as follows: "The school contributes to external courses on mentoring and coaching within professional development and has experience of the use of external mentors and coaches (e.g. from business and industry) for both staff and students. The school is piloting new approaches to mentoring and coaching, such as a system of online student-to-student mentoring and coaching between schools".

[Leading a Self-improving School, David H Hargreaves, NCSL, September 2011]

It is clear, therefore, that coaching and mentoring is vital if schools are serious about developing sustainable leadership (in other words, they wish to 'grow their own leaders') and if schools wish to engage in genuine continuing professional development; but coaching and mentoring is also becoming increasingly important as schools become autonomous of local authority control and move towards the new model of 'teaching schools'. It is vital, too, if they wish to become members of a network of 'family' of schools responsible for developing their own staff and for leading their own programmes of school improvement.

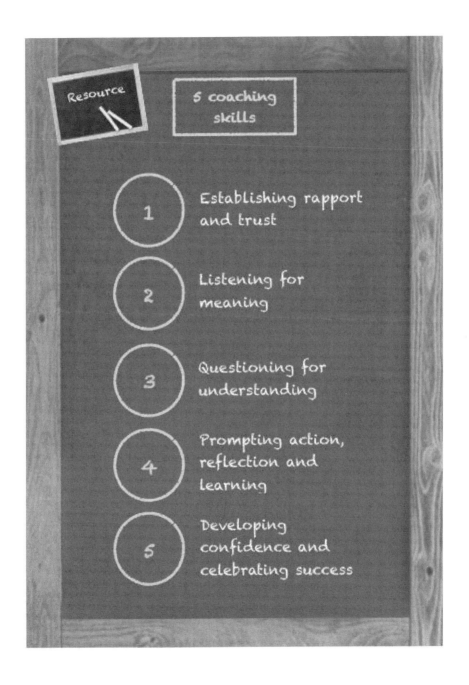

CHAPTER SIX

Managing the business

School leaders are effectively the directors of medium-sized businesses and, as such, they carry a director's responsibility for ensuring that their business is managed according to the law. This is never more important than when managing the school's finances, the school site and the school's digital infrastructure.

It is likely that your school has a finance manager and/or support from your local authority but, nevertheless, the senior team should have a good understanding of the school's budget and should be involved in agreeing its spending priorities - this not only fosters collective responsibility and accountability but also encourages sustainable leadership. Senior leaders should understand how the school's budget is divided and how fiscal decisions are reached.

It is also likely that your school has a site manager or that the responsibility for managing your site is contracted out; but senior leaders should again understand their role in ensuring the school is compliant with health and safety legislation and that the site is kept safe. They should also understand their role with regards to safeguarding – as should every member of staff.

Your school will probably have a network manager and may have an ICT development manager but the senior team should still understand how ICT is used and what the school's priorities are for future ICT developments;

the senior team should also be involved in setting direction when it comes to further investments in the school's digital infrastructure.

Let's look at each of these aspects of managing the business in turn:

Finance

Good financial management can, I believe, be summed up in 3 Ps: prudence, planning, and prioritisation:

Prudence

It is important that school leaders are prudent; it is important that they carefully consider every expense and that they ensure they are achieving value for money. School leaders are accountable for their fiscal decisions and should be confident that any spending they sanction is necessary and represents the best value they can find. Schools need effective processes and procedures in place for contracting, tendering and purchasing. Schools should also have systems in place for producing regular monitoring reports which show the school's current financial position, its future position (budget forecast) and any potential risks.

Planning

School leaders should have a financial plan and this should be linked to the school improvement plan. All the actions on the school improvement plan should, in turn, be costed. Although some costs will be unforeseen, the majority of spending should be planned for. By planning ahead, schools can ensure that their spending will have a long-term impact. Looking ahead and predicting the future is a vital skill for senior leaders. Schools should also have an asset management plan to keep track of their valuable resources and to ensure that those assets are kept serviced and safe.

Prioritisation

When planning the budget, it is important that school leaders prioritise their spending according to the impact the spending will have on students' learning. It is also important that spending is prioritised according to what will have the biggest impact and what will improve most young people's lives.

Balancing the books...

School leaders need to understand where their school's money comes from and how it should be spent. School funding formulas are always changing and they are currently undergoing a sea-change. So I will not linger on the minutiae of income and expenditure, except to say:

Income

The largest proportion of funding is likely to be based on Age Weighted Pupil Units (AWPU). There will be additional funding for aspects such as premises, special needs, local and national initiatives, etc. Post-16 funding is also based on student numbers. Other sources of income include: the pupil premium; extended schools money; lettings.

Expenditure

The single largest expenditure for schools is, by some distance, staffing. Teaching staff are the most costly but do not underestimate the cost of support staff, and clerical and admin staff. Separate but related to staffing is the cost of expenses such as training courses, staff travel and supply teachers. When planning for additional staffing, it is important to include the full costs, including actual salary, as well as national insurance and pension contributions. Other major sources of expenditure include: premises costs such as electricity, gas and water; learning resources such as books, paper, IT hardware and software; supplies and services such as photocopying, catering contractors; the costs of repairs, and health and safety maintenance and inspections such as legionella and PAT testing; and other site costs such as insurance, running a school minibus, and so on.

The school site

The most important aspects of managing the school site are: health and safety and safeguarding.

Health and Safety

In managing health and safety, it is important to ensure that appropriate risk assessments are conducted and implemented, and that systems are in place for identifying and responding to health and safety issues. It is also important that there is a system for ensuring that all accidents are recorded and that action is taken to address issues of concern and to minimise risks. Most health and safety matters can be more easily managed and kept track of if line management responsibilities are clear and all job descriptions include appropriate responsibility for managing health and safety issues. It is also vital that there is a programme of external support and that training is used as appropriate.

Managing health and safety is about:
➢ Coordinating the completion and revision of risk assessments and ensuring they are understood and adhered to
➢ Conducting site checks (usually with a link governor and a contractor or local authority advisor) to ensure the site is safe and to identify areas for improvement such as signage, building repairs and security in order to minimise risks
➢ Developing effective systems for identifying and responding to health and safety issues
➢ Managing the system by which accidents are reported and followed up on
➢ Ensuring fire drills take place termly and a fire log is kept which details each drill and accounts for every fire alarm, fire extinguisher, sprinkler and smoke alarm and records how often they have all been tested
➢ Developing clear accountability, for example by including line management responsibilities in job descriptions
➢ Coordinating a programme of support and training for staff
➢ Providing appropriate first aid provision – both in terms of administering and administrating: in other words, making sure there is appropriate first aid cover, appropriate first aid equipment, and that all instances of first aid are recorded and followed up on
➢ Ensuring there are effective procedures in place for a speedy and safe evacuation of the site in the event of a fire, a loss of power, inclement weather or a bomb threat
➢ Ensuring there is an effective system in place for maintaining the school's physical assets. This means, coordinating a cycle of maintenance, overseeing the testing of equipment (such as PAT testing electrical equipment or testing PE equipment, as well as COSSH testing and testing for legionella)
➢ Managing the school's programme of educational visits, ensuring health and safety and safeguarding checks have been completed, that students' medical needs have been taken care of and that risk assessments have been completed

Safeguarding

Safeguarding has assumed priority status in schools in recent years, not least because of the prominence given to it by Ofsted.

In her commentary to Ofsted's 2009/10 Annual Report, Her Majesty's Chief Inspector wrote:

> 'Safeguarding…is an issue addressed not only with increasing sureness by those responsible for keeping children and learners safe, but one felt keenly by those most vulnerable to harm and neglect.'

It is right that safeguarding should be viewed with such importance because there can be no issue of greater import to parents and carers, or indeed to schools, than the safety of their children. Although the Ofsted framework has changed and the number of judgment areas has been slashed, safeguarding continues to feature strongly in the 2012 inspection schedule – not least in the judgment of behaviour and safety and as a subheading of the leadership and management judgment.

But what is safeguarding?

The definition used in the Children Act 2004 and in the Department for Education guidance document *Working together to safeguard children*, (which focuses on safeguarding and promoting children's and learners' welfare), can be summarised as follows:
- protecting children and learners from maltreatment
- preventing impairment of children's and learners' health or development
- ensuring that children and learners are growing up in circumstances consistent with the provision of safe and effective care
- undertaking that role so as to enable those children and learners to have optimum life chances and to enter adulthood successfully.

The governing bodies of maintained schools and local authorities must comply with the Education Act 2002. The Department for Education guidance, *Safeguarding children and safer recruitment in education,* makes it clear that **schools must provide a safe environment and take action to identify and protect any children or young people who are at risk of significant harm.**

Schools are required:
- to prevent unsuitable people from working with children and young people;
- to promote safe practice and challenge unsafe practice;
- to ensure that staff receive the necessary training for their roles; and
- to work in partnership with other agencies providing services for children and young people.
- Local authorities have a duty:
- to provide model policies and procedures on all aspects of safeguarding;
- to ensure that schools are aware of, and comply with, their responsibilities.

In evaluating the effectiveness of safeguarding in schools, Ofsted inspectors focus on a broad range of issues including:
- the impact of safeguarding arrangements on outcomes for pupils, including staying safe, being healthy, making a positive contribution, enjoying and achieving, and developing skills for economic well-being
- how well pupils are taught to keep themselves safe
- how well the school protects pupils from bullying, racist abuse, harassment or discrimination, and promotes good behaviour
- the effectiveness of health and safety policies and procedures, including conducting necessary risk assessments as well as regular checks on equipment and premises
- the effectiveness of arrangements to provide a safe environment and a secure school site
- how well the school meets the needs of pupils with medical conditions
- how appropriately child welfare and child protection concerns are identified and responded to by the school
- how effectively the school works with key agencies to safeguard and promote the welfare of children
- how well the school prioritises safeguarding, and monitors and evaluates the effectiveness of its policies and practices
- the extent to which the school ensures that adults working with children are appropriately recruited and vetted, and receive appropriate training, guidance, support and supervision to undertake the effective safeguarding of pupils.

Ofsted produced a 'good practice' report in September 2011 which identified the features of exceptionally good safeguarding and its findings are worth considering here. Ofsted say that there is no reason why good practice in safeguarding should not be a feature of every school; the practice described in its report is replicable in every school. Its features of best practice not only comply with the legal requirements but often move beyond them. Safeguarding, as detailed in their report, is not seen as a burden but as a "reasonable and essential part of the fabric of the school".

The report pays attention to the "meticulous and systematic implementation of policies and routines" but shows how it should also involve every member of the school community.

19% of the schools who contributed to the report were judged to be outstanding in their safeguarding procedures in 2009/10.

The key word when it comes to safeguarding for both inspectors and schools is 'reasonable' and it is around the interpretation of 'reasonable' that a mythology has emerged. In the report, Ofsted attempts to set the record straight:

> "Ofsted does not require schools to build walls around play areas; it does not expect schools to seek Criminal Records Bureau checks on casual visitors to schools, including parents; it does not judge a school to be inadequate because of minor administrative errors, or because an inspector's ID was not checked. Ofsted does not try to 'catch schools out'."

Key features of outstanding practice in safeguarding

Here, in summary form, are the findings of the Ofsted report. Most of the features of outstanding practice are found, to a greater or lesser extent, in all effective schools with outstanding safeguarding arrangements:

➢ high-quality leadership and management that makes safeguarding a priority across all aspects of a school's work
➢ stringent vetting procedures in place for staff and other adults
➢ rigorous safeguarding policies and procedures in place, written in plain English, compliant with statutory requirements and updated regularly; in particular, clear and coherent child protection policies
➢ child protection arrangements that are accessible to everyone, so that pupils and families, as well as adults in the school, know who they can talk to if they are worried
➢ excellent communication systems with up-to-date information that can be accessed and shared by those who need it
➢ a high priority given to training in safeguarding, generally going beyond basic requirements, extending expertise widely and building internal capacity

➤ robust arrangements for site security, understood and applied by staff and pupils
➤ a curriculum that is flexible, relevant and engages pupils' interest; that is used to promote safeguarding, not least through teaching pupils how to stay safe, how to protect themselves from harm and how to take responsibility for their own and others' safety
➤ courteous and responsible behaviour by the pupils, enabling everyone to feel secure and well-protected
➤ well thought out and workable day-to-day arrangements to protect and promote pupils' health and safety
➤ rigorous monitoring of absence, with timely and appropriate follow-up, to ensure that pupils attend regularly
➤ risk assessment taken seriously and used to good effect in promoting safety.

[Ofsted, 2011]

Digital Infrastructure

In 2006, Christine Gilbert wrote to the secretary of state for education on behalf of the Teaching and Learning 2020 Review Group outlining what teaching and learning might look like in our schools in the year 2020. Her report outlined what schools needed to do if they were to meet the needs of young people in the 21st Century. She talked about the need to personalise learning by "focusing in a more structured way on each child's learning in order to enhance progress, achievement and participation".

The group's report started with a few sobering thoughts: it stated that:
➤ In 2020, the children who started in Reception classes in September 2006 will be entering higher education or employment. Fourteen years is one entire school generation.
➤ Most new school leaders in 2020 are now [this was 2006] in their early years of teaching or still studying.
➤ Many of the parents of the children who will start primary education in 2020 are just coming to the end of their own schooling.

The review group set out what they saw as the main drivers of change – the five things they said would drive major changes in society and, therefore, five foci for schools to take account of between 2006 and 2020. These drivers were:

Demographic: there will be more over-65s than under-16s in 2020 although, after a decline, the primary-age population will be expanding. The teaching profession, on average, is likely to be younger and less experienced. While there are concerns about the health of the current generation of children and young people, generally people will be living and experiencing better health for longer. We expect to see even greater ethnic diversity, with further concentrations of minority ethnic groups in particular geographical areas.

Social: We expect to see a greater diversity of social attitudes and expectations and a decline in 'traditional' family structures – although not in 'family values'. Alongside social diversity will be greater religious diversity, although England will be a more secular country overall. These trends are likely to result in increasing involvement in 'single interest' politics. A greater proportion of children will have parents who were educated to university level. Gender inequality will continue to decline gradually. There is no evidence that the increasing incidence of child and adolescent mental health disorders seen over the last few decades is likely to diminish.

Technological: The pace of technological change will continue to increase exponentially. Increases in 'bandwidth' will lead to a rise in internet-based services, particularly access to video and television. Costs associated with hardware, software and data storage will decrease further. This is likely to result in near-universal access to personal, multi-functional devices, smarter software integrated with global standards and increasing amounts of information being available to search on line (with faster search engines). Using ICT will be natural for most pupils and for an increasing majority of teachers.

Economic: We expect living standards to be around 30% higher, with more 'luxuries' becoming 'necessities' and a greater proportion of income spent on leisure, household services, sport and culture. Higher level skills will be emphasised within a knowledge-based economy: a loss of 'mid-range' occupations will mean that young people will need to be better qualified to secure employment. Working patterns will be increasingly diverse and occupational structures less hierarchical. Workplace skills will change, requiring employees to be flexible and adaptable.

Environmental: A heightened awareness of threats to the environment and the need for responsible, decisive action to counter them will mean that individuals will be expected to take personal responsibility for their impact on the environment; they will expect public services and the private sector to do likewise.

[Teaching and Learning 2020 Review Group, 2006]

One of the key drivers of change is technology: the group predicted that using ICT would be natural for most students and for most teachers by 2020. It also predicted that the economy would be knowledge-based. But at their heart, all five 'drivers' are concerned with technology: technology is changing the world students will inhabit; and technology is changing the way students learn in order to be prepared for this new world.

The report went on to say that:

> During their school years, children should grow from relative dependence on their parents and teachers into mature learners, with the skills to adapt to changing demands. Society's aspirations for them are expressed in the outcomes of the Every Child Matters framework: be healthy, stay safe, enjoy and achieve, make a positive contribution and achieve economic well-being. Our vision is one in which these aspirations are realised for all children and young people. The education system will need to act now if it is to transform the experience of children starting school today. We do not underestimate the challenges involved. However, we believe that the process of achieving our vision will be an exciting one in which many schools are already leading the way.

> Together, schools, local and national government need to work towards a society in which:
> - a child's chances of success are not related to his or her socio-economic background, gender or ethnicity
> - education services are designed around the needs of each child, with the expectation that all learners achieve high standards
> - all children and young people leave school with functional skills in English and mathematics, understanding how to learn, think creatively, take risks and handle change
> - teachers use their skills and knowledge to engage children and young people as partners in learning, acting quickly to adjust their teaching in response to pupils' learning
> - schools draw in parents as their child's co-educators, engaging them and increasing their capacity to support their child's learning.

> We believe that personalising learning and teaching must play a central role in transforming England's education service to achieve these aims between now and 2020

And the report places significant weight on the part that new technologies have to play in realising this 20:20 vision. It says:

> Already, with significant government investment, over the past ten years the use of technology in schools has increased considerably. The new technologies have an impact on a school in three main areas:
> - o   the administration of the school, including budgeting, planning and databases managing pupil details and progress

- the creation and delivery of lesson materials, including teachers' and pupils' use of whiteboards, visualisers, handheld voting devices and tablet PCs to enable reproduction of and access to resources
- the use of domestic digital technology as a learning tool, including home access to the internet, digital cameras, video cameras, gaming devices, Personal Digital Assistants (PDAs) and mobile phones.

"New technologies," the report continues, "contribute to personalising learning by influencing what, how and why children learn" by:

- broadening the range of learning material children are able to access, either guided by a teacher or as part of self-directed learning
- enabling quick interactive assessments, for example, using 'voting' technology promoting development of a broad range of knowledge, skills and understanding, in new contexts and with virtual access to experts
- facilitating collaboration with peers (in the same school and in other schools)
- increasing the variety of learning resources, software and communication tools, through new media
- helping schools to use a wider range of readily available resources and software to enhance learning, including making software available to children to use at home
- blurring distinctions between informal and formal learning – giving children the ability to choose what they learn and when they learn it
- increasing motivation, through pace and variety
- increased relevance, through greater links between children's experience of school and of the technology-rich world outside.

And the success of ICT can be supported by:

- Engagement with parents and pupils - expanding the potential for communication, sharing resources, creating shared spaces to record pupils' learning and progress
- Whole-school systems - integrated learning and management systems that bring together all the information on pupils' progress and analysis of assessment data, and are capable of being shared with other schools and organisations

It is clear, therefore, that ICT is not just about supporting students' learning. It is about supporting teachers and others to monitor and track student progress, as well as report to parents. The report says that, "While all schools have systems for recording and reporting information about pupils and their achievement, this information is not always readily available to those who could draw on it to improve learning, namely classroom teachers, pupils, and parents. Using the new technologies to inform learning and teaching will be a priority. This should take advantage of the potential of on-line learning opportunities linked to individual learning plans (or 'e-portfolios') and information held on pupils' progress."

As an Assistant Headteacher responsible for teaching and learning at the time the report was published, I decided to conduct my own research on the subject. I asked my teaching staff to describe the average school classroom now [2007] and predict what the school classroom of 2020 would be like by comparison. This is what they said:

By 2020, learning in our classrooms will:

1. Be more independent; more personalised and less age-based (students will take exams when they're ready not when they're the right age)
2. Offer more curriculum breadth and choice
3. Be more focused on what employers want; encourage more involvement from employers
4. Be focused on developing transferrable skills
5. Be focused on how to lead healthier lifestyles
6. Be focused on multi-cultural issues
7. Use ICT more often and more appropriately, including personal laptops for all, the use of podcasts, the use of virtual learning environments (VLE) and the use of video-conferencing
8. Account for the fact that students are more streetwise
9. Account for the fact that students are more dependent on technology
10. Place a greater emphasis on teaching to learn NOT teaching to the test
11. Reflect the change in the types of careers available
12. Be more vocational e.g. courses for electricians, plumbers, etc.
13. Place a greater emphasis on teaching life skills such as financial capability
14. Involve fewer physical books
15. Account for students' shorter attention spans due to the overuse of technology
16. Account for the greater prevalence of drugs and alcohol
17. Place a greater emphasis on the importance of communication skills

Again, the dominant feature in my rather crude piece of research was this certain belief that schools would respond best to the learning needs of students in the 21st Century by using technology more and by using it more effectively.

It follows, therefore, that ICT is a vital resource for school leaders to manage.

Developing ICT in schools is often underestimated: it is assumed that using ICT simply means using an interactive whiteboard. All too often, schools take a single-minded approach to ICT - they assume effective ICT solely means teachers using ICT in lessons (and overusing new technologies); they view ICT as a panacea and use it every lesson. This has several negative effects: not least, 'death by Powerpoint'! If a new technology is over-used, students become apathetic towards it and are less engaged in their learning. If technology is used for the sake of it when more traditional means of teaching would be better, the key learning is lost amidst the 'light show'.

ICT is about much more than using interactive whiteboards. Indeed, ICT should be used to:
- Promote social interaction
- Support inclusion
- Provide a safe environment
- Enable students to track their own progress
- Enable parents to engage with school
- Motivate staff
- Enable teachers to create resources
- Support planning
- Support target-setting, assessment and reporting
- Support school improvement planning, and monitoring and reviewing performance
- Allow for efficient administration and to reduce bureaucracy

ICT should be seen as a vital tool not just for teachers in the classroom but for the admin team, for middle and senior leaders, and for parents and governors. ICT shouldn't be viewed simply as a learning resource but should be seen as a means of improving efficiency and reducing bureaucracy. It should also be seen as a means of tracking student progress, of tracking school improvement, and of extending the boundaries of learning beyond the school gates.

If ICT is to be used effectively and in these diverse ways, school leaders should consider the following challenges when developing ICT in schools:

Safeguarding
How do schools ensure that children are protected and kept safe whilst using ICT?

Inclusion
How do schools ensure that the use of ICT is differentiated?

Good value for money
How do schools ensure that ICT is affordable and has long-term benefits?

Home access
How do schools ensure every student has fair access and that they extend the boundaries of learning for every child? How do they ensure parental engagement?

(The eagle-eyed among you will have spotted another mnemonic: SIGH.)

If we take SIGH as our list of ICT challenges, our priorities for ICT development should, therefore, be:
- Promoting student entitlement and encouraging the use of ICT for learning
- Ensuring universal – and safe – access in and out of school
- Developing appropriate professional tools and providing training for staff
- Developing a cost-effective, reliable digital infrastructure and having in place effective contingency plans for when that infrastructure fails

School leaders, therefore, have the duty to manage the school's digital infrastructure. They should have a long-term vision for the way ICT is used in order to promote student progress and to reduce bureaucracy for staff. ICT should form part of the school improvement plan - as an objective in its own right and as a means of achieving other objectives.

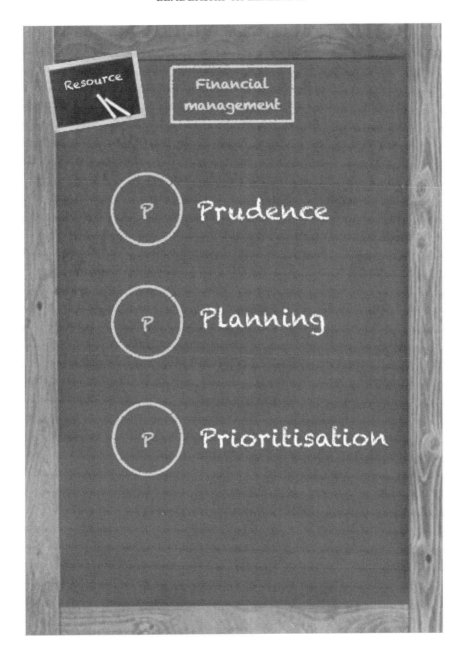

CHAPTER SEVEN

Working with stakeholders

Working with governors

Naturally, the model of governance employed at your school depends on the type of school you work in. Some schools are controlled by the local authority; others are controlled by a diocese or by sponsors; new 'free schools' are controlled by myriad groups of interested persons including parents and media personalities. But, whatever type of school you work in, it will have a governing body.

The relationship between the senior team and the governing body is vital if a school is to become outstanding. School leaders need to understand the role of the governing body and governors need to appreciate what they are and are not permitted to do. The lines need to be drawn. A simple rule of thumb when demarcating roles and responsibilities is this:

> ➢ Governors are concerned with strategy
> ➢ School leaders are concerned with leadership and management

But school governance is an odd thing: the distinction between school leaders and governors can easily become blurred; it is not always clear where the real power lies, and where support and challenge cross over into direction and command. Some governing bodies are passive and trust their headteacher to run the school how he or she sees fit, relying on the local authority to provide the appropriate checks and balances. Other governing bodies are active and hold the headteacher firmly to account; they scrutinise every decision and pore over performance data and the school budget with keen eyes.

My own view is this: governors are akin to a board of non-executive directors in a company - they work for the school and should be champions of it, speaking highly of the school within the local community and protecting its best interests; governors are not independent arbiters or representatives of community interests or constituents.

It is true that governing bodies exist to provide strategic leadership and to be the accountable body. It's also true, therefore, that they need to be able to support and challenge the senior team's decisions. To do this, they need to be kept informed and they need to understand where the school is going. But this challenge should not extend to public criticisms of the school. It is not uncommon for a chair of governors and headteacher to disagree over key decisions and for there to ensue a robust, often bitter, dispute. These disputes are not always entirely unhealthy, either. A headteacher needs challenge and if his or her decision cannot be justified to the chair of governors then it is just possible that it is a bad decision.

Equally, a head should be able to question the governing body's decisions and/or perceptions and make them see the reality of a situation. It is the head, not the governors, who works in the school every day and has the better understanding of what works and what does not work. It is the head, not the governors, who knows his or her staff best and has a duty of care towards them. But disagreements between a headteacher and a chair of governors should be kept private - private from the community and private from other school staff - because it is important for morale that governors and senior leaders are seen to have one voice, are seen to be working in unison. Public disagreements or disparaging remarks by governors can be damaging not only to the school's reputation but also to staff morale - which, in turn, could hamper performance and therefore be a self-fulfilling prophecy.

It is equally important that the headteacher respects his governing body and involves governors in key decision-making. It is also important that he or she keeps his governing body informed on a regular basis - not least because this is something Ofsted look for in the new framework: governance is now consumed within the overall Leadership and Management judgment and so no matter how effective the senior team is, the school cannot be judged good or outstanding for Leadership and Management if its governing body is not genuinely involved and regularly informed.

What is the governing body's role?

Governors are about strategy and need to work with senior leaders on agreeing the school's direction of travel, on agreeing the school's priorities going forward, and on agreeing the key objectives in the school improvement plan.

In particular, governors are responsible for the strategic leadership of:
➢ School finances
➢ Staffing and personnel (including appointing new staff, reorganising and restructuring existing staff such as reassigning leadership and TLR responsibilities)
➢ Discipline and pastoral care
➢ The performance management of the headteacher
➢ The curriculum plan
➢ SEN provision
➢ School buildings and their environment (including health and safety and safeguarding)
➢ Admissions policy and decisions
➢ Target-setting procedures
➢ The SEF
➢ The school improvement plan
➢ Aspects of self-evaluation

Governors are not about day-to-day management: this remains the responsibility of the senior team and other school personnel.

It is important that senior leaders and governors support and respect each other and empathise with each other's roles. Senior leaders should never forget that (in most cases, though the government is considering changes to this) governors are unpaid volunteers who dedicate a lot of their own time to helping the school and they do so because they genuinely care about the school and about the young people in its care. Equally, governors should never forget that senior leaders are paid to take difficult decisions and are appointed on the basis that they have demonstrated the capacity and ability to lead a school. Accordingly, they should be afforded the time and space to lead the school effectively.

This delicate balance is best struck through a clarity of procedures and policies. Systems and structures need to be in place to make clear everyone's roles and to ensure everyone performs those roles effectively or is appropriately challenged if they fall short of what is expected of them.

Senior leaders should develop good working relationships with governors, especially the chairs of the various governors' committees through which important information can be fed. Link governors should also act as conduits of information and as such they need to develop effective working relationships with their link middle and senior leaders, relationships based on mutual respect and trust. Link governors for some areas may need to make regular contact and be voracious in challenging their link member of staff for his or her decisions and actions; other link governors - secure in the improvements made by their link member of staff and by that person's knowledge, skills and experience - can step back and need only provide support when it is asked for.

Senior leaders should also provide key briefing documents to governors in order to assist governors in making important strategic decisions: this can best be achieved by leaders providing high quality summaries or headline data (not long, detailed reports) and a set of reasoned options for governors to debate and decide upon. These documents should be distributed in advance of decision-making meetings to allow thoughtful consideration and to avoid protracted discussions.

In addition to providing strategic leadership to those areas of school listed above, governors are also responsible for the following ongoing tasks:

Monitoring the school improvement plan - this can be done through the headteacher's report, through discussions at governors' meetings and/or via reports and data analysis from school leaders including heads of department.

Visiting the school - visits are likely to be made at key times such as during interviews, appraisals, and at times of uncertainty and change; governors are also likely to visit the school to attend important events such as presentations and open evenings.

Making link visits - governors are likely to be linked to the curriculum, pastoral or admin areas for which they are accountable and should meet with their link contact at key points in the year (though, as I say above, the nature and frequency of such visits should be tailored to suit the context): some departments need a 'light touch' because they are thriving - such visits might therefore be about recognising and celebrating achievement; others might need closer attention.

The key to an effective working relationship between senior leaders and the governing body is for both parties to be open and honest and to keep the other informed. There is nothing to be gained by keeping secrets or being duplicitous. Both parties should also remember that they are on the same side and should find ways of working together for the benefit of the school.

In situations where the headteacher and chair of governors struggle to build an effective working relationship, it is important that both parties remain professional. Heads also need to recognise that the government has given governors a more formal role which might not suit what the head wants or is used to. It may be necessary to bring in a critical friend, someone who will mediate a conversation between the headteacher and either the chair or the whole governing body. One strategy the critical friend could employ is to carry out a governors' self-review exercise to look at what's working well and what could be improved about the way the governing body works. That will help bring issues out into the open in a 'safe' way. It may also be useful for the critical friend to write down sets of expectations for both sides, to talk through them so that, in the end, there are no unfounded assumptions being made on either side about what each can expect. Furthermore, policies, procedures and an agreed code of conduct can help ensure that everyone abides by the same rules.

Working with parents

I have heard it said that parents are a school's customers. I disagree with this analogy. The relationship between a school and its students' parents is much more complex than that between a company and its customers. Yes, a school provides a service to its parents but that service is one of the most important services imaginable: that of securing a good future for their sons and daughters. Indeed, what could be more important - other than a child's health - than a child's education. But schools are not beholden to parents, they do not exist to serve parents. Often a school knows better than a parent what is in the best interests of the student (and I am speaking as a father of three). Often a school has to challenge and question a parent's behaviour or beliefs. Often a school has to say difficult and unpopular things or refer a parent to the police or social services. No, the relationship between a school and its parents is more complex than that.

The relationship between schools and parents should be built on mutual trust and respect but this can often be hard-fought. The best starting point for school leaders when forging this relationship is to consider how their school is going to engage with parents. As ever, I have a mnemonic to help capture the key points... dealing with parents should be about staying CALM:

C   Calm and quiet and patient
A   Action to be promised within appropriate timescales
L   Listen carefully and take notes
M   Make decisions based on all the evidence & for the good of the school

School leaders should always stay calm and talk quietly to parents. Sometimes it may be necessary to remove a parent from a place of conflict. It is important that school leaders remember that they are a role model - the professional - and should lead by example. Accordingly, they should not respond to a parent's aggression by raising their voices nor should they be intimidated by foul language.

School leaders are gatekeepers for their staff: they should protect their staff and should not let a parent see a teacher until there is a reduction in the aggression (and even then it may not be the best course of action). It is worth adopting a clear policy regarding meetings with teachers which has the following caveat at its heart: a teacher's first duty is to teach his or her classes and not to meet with parents; appointments, therefore, have to be arranged in advance and parents without prior appointments will not be seen. Instead of referring parents to the classroom teacher, senior leaders should listen to the parent personally (when the parent has become calm) and note the nature of the complaint. They should allow the parent a reasonable amount of time to articulate their grievance and should avoid interrupting because this may aggravate the situation further. Of course, this has to be balanced with the senior leader's need to utilise their own time effectively and perform their other duties. Once they have listened, they should summarise the key points as they understand them and ask for clarification on any points of confusion. Then they should promise to gather together all the information they will need in order to make a comprehensive and fair assessment of the matter.

Senior leaders should not immediately side with or agree with the parent or the teacher. Nor should they promise any specific action. Rather, they should promise to phone or meet with the parent again at an agreed time - ideally within a couple of days - in order to take the matter forward. The school leader should then investigate the circumstances with the appropriate members of staff, look for a fair and just solution and see how both parties can be brought together to resolve the matter. Any action should be taken with the best interests of the school in mind: the right decision for the majority of students may not be what the parent wants you to do, nor what the teacher wants you to do. You should be confident that you are taking the right decision in the circumstances and once all the facts are known, and you should be confident that your decision will stand up to scrutiny over the long-term. Of course, depending on the severity of the incident, it may be advisable to consult with other senior colleagues or your headteacher or, if you are the headteacher, your chair of governors or local authority advisor.

In order to avoid confrontation from arising in the first place, your school should have a clear policy for dealing with parents which is known to and understood by all parents. Firstly, it should set out what you expect parents to do. For example:

> We encourage parents to:
> o   be supportive,
> o   be informed,
> o   maintain a direct involvement in their child's progress,
> o   understand what the school is trying to achieve for their child,
> o   take a positive position - contribute to initiatives like home visits and
>   information-gathering events such as parents' consultation evenings,
> o   visit school and be informed about issues and initiatives,
> o   support events that promote the school efforts,
> o   be aware of and support any home/school agreements.

Your parental engagement policy should also outline how your school intends to communicate with parents and how it will consult with parents on key decisions. It may be useful to start with a statement of intent such as this:

> Our school, in order to be effective, must acknowledge, appreciate and respond to the views of parents. It needs to take informed decisions following consultation processes.

Your school will communicate with parents in a variety of ways including:
- parents' consultation evenings
- open evenings
- information meetings
- parents' workshops and discussion forums
- parents' associations or committees
- formal questionnaires and market research products
- regular newsletters
- the school website
- on-line reporting and parents portal
- text messaging
- email

Your school will need a clear strategy for communicating effectively and expediently in each of these circumstances.

As well as writing letters (your school should have a policy dictating your 'house style' and letters should be checked and formatted by the admin team), it is likely you will use email and text messaging to communicate with parents. Before relying on email and texts to impart important information, it is vital you understand access arrangements: do all parents have Internet and cellular coverage and do all parents have the financial means to utilise it? Will you disadvantage some parents if you rely solely on email and texts? You may need to adopt a 'belt and braces' approach to communication by sending a text and/or email to indicate that a letter is on its way. And what of the school website? Your school should have a policy explaining how it will use its website to aid communication. It is likely it will be used for publishing news articles, celebrating school successes and reproducing the school calendar. It may also - and to be an outstanding school which extends the boundaries of learning, it should - use the website for setting work and for providing help and advice to students. The website may provide an overview of each course and syllabus being taught in school and may have links to homework tasks and extension tasks should students and parents wish to do extra work in order to secure the learning or to revise. As well as a policy for how your school communicates with parents, it will need a policy for how staff use these means of communication to ensure accuracy, timeliness and appropriateness.

Working with the community

In Chapter One I state that senior leaders should develop and encourage effective partnerships with other schools, agencies and the community. I also opine that community cohesion is frequently misunderstood or underestimated: it is solely seen as being about offering the school site to the local community. And, yes, encouraging community use of your school is important (be it leasing your fields to the local football team or running adult education classes in the evenings). But community cohesion is also about respecting diversity and protecting vulnerable learners; it is about better understanding the local community and taking account of where students come from; it is about working with parents; it is about bringing world issues into schools in order to raise students' awareness of the world around them; it is about responding to the Every Child Matters agenda and respecting diversity and inclusion of all types, ensuring every child has the opportunity to fulfil his or her potential irrespective of where they come from and what means they have.

Community cohesion, therefore, is about:

➤ tracking vulnerable groups to ensure all students make good progress
➤ using the school for community events
➤ developing an international dimension through exchange programmes or special events
➤ developing an effective inclusion policy which includes arrangements for student induction

Why? Because community cohesion is strongest when:

1. Systems for student tracking ensure that student progress is carefully monitored for all groups of learners including vulnerable students such as those on free school meals, those with special educational needs and those from ethnic minorities or challenging backgrounds;
2. The school is seen as a community hub and the community feels a part of the school - it is committed to helping the school to improve and celebrates its successes;
3. There is some sort of international dimension to the work of the school which informs students about what is happening in the world around them, and encourages them to be more understanding and empathetic towards other cultures;
4. There is an effective inclusion policy which promotes genuine inclusivity for all learners and there is an appropriate induction process for new students and their families which makes them feel welcome, makes them feel a part of the school 'family' and makes them feel able to contribute to school life.

A school should actively seek partnerships with its community in order to provide enrichment opportunities. For example, partnerships with local businesses might open doors to school trips and work experience placements. It might also encourage local business leaders and entrepreneurs to visit school to give talks or to assist with mock interviews and CV writing workshops. Schools should encourage community leaders to attend and contribute to school events on a regular basis.

The school, in turn, should endeavour to make a contribution to community groups that support vulnerable people, and the school should support the wider community through charitable activities and fund-raising events. Perhaps the school could become involved in a community project.

Schools should involve their local community in their work by keeping them informed about school events and successes through newsletters, the local media, and their web site. They should invest time and thought into how they market their successes within the community because to do so is vital to raising the school's profile. Raising the school's profile is, in turn, vital to making the school an attractive proposition to new students and families, and to ensuring it remains highly thought of. And, as I say in the introduction, message is important!

C	Calm and quiet and patient
A	Action to be promised within appropriate timescales
L	Listen carefully and take notes
M	Make decisions based on all the evidence and for the good of school

M J BROMLEY

BIBLIOGRAPHY

As a senior leader working in schools every day, it has been necessary for me to keep abreast of the latest pedagogical thinking and research, as well as government policy and procedure. I have read countless publications from the Department for Education and its various quangos, as well as Ofsted and the various teaching unions. I have also read a significant proportion of the National College for School Leadership's impressive output. It is not possible to give credit to all of these documents and their authors here but, undoubtedly, my ideas have been influenced by a great number of organisations and people to whom I owe a debt of gratitude.

I cite some specific reports in this series (from Ofsted, for example) that I will not needlessly reproduce here. However, the following publications have made a significant contribution to the contents of this book and I feel they deserve a special mention. I would recommend you read them yourself – most are freely available in the public domain:

Creasy, Jane & Paterson, Fred; **Leading Coaching in Schools**, National College for School Leadership [2005]

Gilbert, C & various; 2020 **Vision: Report of the Teaching and Learning in 2020 Review Group**, Crown Copyright [2006]

Hargreaves, D H; **Leading a Self-Improving School**, National College for School Leadership [2011]

Lofthouse, R; Leat, D; Towler, C; **Coaching for Teaching and Learning**, CfBT Education Trust [2010]

Various contributors; **Little Book of Change**, Training & Development Agency for Schools [2008]

Various contributors; **National Framework for Mentoring and Coaching**, CUREE [2005]

I also refer to:

Furlong, J; Maynard, T; **Mentoring Student Teachers**, London Routledge [1995]

M J BROMLEY

FURTHER READING

I do not mention or cite the following publications but would recommend them as further reading:

Dougill, P; Raleigh, M; Blatchford, R; Fryer, L; Robinson, C; Richmond, J; **To the next level: good schools becoming outstanding**, CfBT Education Trust [2011]

Lewis, P; Murphy, R; **Effective School Leadership**, National College for School Leadership [2008]

ABOUT THE AUTHOR

M. J. Bromley is an education consultant and writer.

He was Deputy Headteacher (and Acting Headteacher) of the highest performing comprehensive school in its authority and one of the top five most improved schools in England, a school Ofsted judged 'good with outstanding features' under their new framework.

He now works with Solutions for School, an education consultancy group which supports secondary schools across the UK. He also works with Creative Education as a consultant Headteacher and lecturer, and with Pearson Publishing developing school improvement resources. He is an associate with Evolving Literacy (a company which helps English faculties to improve planning and assessment), an assessor for three exam boards, and writes on education for The Guardian.

He has fifteen years' senior leadership experience in the public and private sectors including over eight years on the leadership team of two schools: one a large inner-city school, the other a small rural school. Prior to teaching, he was a senior manager in the telecoms industry; he has also worked in journalism. He has an Honours degree in English Language and Literature, a Post-Graduate Certificate in Education and the National Professional Qualification for Headship.

He lives in Yorkshire with his wife and their three children.

ALSO BY THE AUTHOR

Ofsted: Thriving Not Surviving Under the 2012 Framework

The IQ Myth: How To Grow Your Own Intelligence

A Teacher's Guide To... Behaviour Management

FORTHCOMING TITLES BY THE AUTHOR

In this series:

Assessment for Learning
Behaviour for Learning
Curriculum for Learning
Future for Learning

In the 'A Teacher's Guide To...' series:

A Teacher's Guide To... Personalised Learning
A Teacher's Guide To... Assessment

Under the 2012 Framework

The Blurb

"A practical, hands-on book written in a fluent, friendly style which makes it easy and enjoyable to read. It makes sense of what is a difficult job and cuts through some complex ideas and issues and makes them accessible."
- Assistant Headteacher

"This book is readable and engaging. It manages to draw you in almost immediately and you find yourself reading on and on, appreciating how one can make a difference."
School Business Manager

'Ofsted: Thriving Not Surviving Under the 2012 Framework' is a useful quick-read for all school leaders but is essential reading for leaders who have not yet experienced an inspection under the new framework.

This book provides a practical walk-through of the new inspection process and is full of helpful advice about how to ensure a smooth, successful visit.

It deftly summarises the new framework as well as the changes expected to come into force in September 2012 including 'almost no-notice inspections'.

The book covers: the new framework; what to do before an inspection; what to do during an inspection; what to do after an inspection; the implications of 'almost no-notice' inspections; Ofsted are not the reason we do what we do.

Available on from www.solutionsforschool.co.uk.

The IQ Myth:
How To Grow Your Own Intelligence

The Blurb

Alfred Binet invented the IQ test - not as a measure of innate intellect or ability, nor as a number by which someone's capabilities could be determined - but as a way of identifying children who were not profiting from the Paris public school system. Binet, far from believing IQ was a measure of natural-born talent, said that anyone could achieve anything with "practice, training, and above all, method".

Taking these three words - uttered a century ago - as its premise, "The IQ Myth" explores the importance of hard work and practice - rather than innate ability or intellect - in improving one's intelligence. Primarily written for school teachers - though a fascinating book for anyone interested in the science of how we learn - "The IQ Myth" examines the true nature of intelligence and argues that nurture is more important than nature when it comes to realising one's potential.

"The IQ Myth" argues that teachers who 'dumb down' and expect students to make little or no progress get just that in return: 'dumb' students who make little or no progress. However, teachers who set challenging, aspirational targets and push their students to be the best they can be, teachers who create an atmosphere in which students truly believe they can make progress and exceed expectations, get results.

Building on the work of a range of psychologists and social commenters including Alfred Binet, Carol Dweck, Daniel Pink, Malcolm Gladwell, Matthew Syed and Daniel Goleman, this book looks at a range of so-called geniuses (from Thomas Edison to Mozart) and sportspeople (from Michael Jordan to this year's Tour de France winner Bradley Wiggins) and questions the real secret of success and the damaging effect of praise.

Intellectually challenging but written in a friendly, fluent style, this book is a fascinating quick-read for anyone interested in the nature of talent and an essential read for school teachers who want to motivate their students to get better results.

Available from <u>www.solutionsforschool.co.uk</u>.

SOLUTIONS *for* SCHOOL

www.solutionsforschool.co.uk

Follow us on Twitter: @solution4school

Find us on Facebook: www.facebook.com/bromleyeducation

Email us to find out how we can help you improve your processes of school improvement and self-evaluation: solutionsforschool@gmail.com

Printed in Great Britain
by Amazon.co.uk, Ltd.,
Marston Gate.